Happiness Struggles?

Don Barnes

Published by Don Barnes, 2024.

This publication provides the Author's opinion and neither the publisher or the author intends to render legal, accounting, or other professional advice with this publication.
The publisher and the author disclaim any personal liability, loss or risk incurred as a consequence of the use and application, directly or indirectly, of advice, information or methods presented in this publication.

First Edition

Table of Contents

About the Author

Don is the founder and author of Life Works in Threes!™ E-books. He is a lifelong Texan who has traveled extensively while taking a keen interest in human behavior. His curiosity about life and what drives humans led him to the discovery of how life works in threes. He coined this term as the *Tryune Concept.*

Don attended college on an athletic scholarship and then embarked on a 30-year career in the oil and gas industry. Since the year 2000, he has been a consultant for distributors and manufacturers of various industries. Along the way, he worked on his Tryune discovery in hopes of someday sharing his findings with those struggling unnecessarily... in life. What Don surmised from 40+ years of R&D was that people were struggling unnecessarily because they were not aware that "life works in threes." They, for the most part, have been living their lives <u>by chance</u> rather than <u>by choice,</u> he also discovered.

From this, he began focusing on the "mechanics of life" which shows formulas for success with subjects such as *life, health, money, purpose and so forth.* When people are able to grasp the Tryune Concept, they can apply the formulas with topics that interest them and begin eliminating the struggle. This epiphany is what triggered his Tryune venture and is now on the path of sharing with all who desire to improve on their lives.

Don currently resides in Southern California and Texas while overseeing his businesses and investments.

Life Works in Threes™

When I was a kid growing up, no one sat me down and said, "Okay Don, I'm going to show you how life works so that you can navigate your way through adulthood." I graduated from school, got married and went about my way with the "learn as you go" concept. It was kind of like putting together a backyard swing set without a set of instructions. Lots of frustration and do-overs, for sure!

My discovery of the "triune" word and noticing how things come together in threes is really what set me off on researching that maybe "life comes in three" ...sort of a mechanical approach to managing life, if you will. I combed the libraries and bookstores for information on this and found one book on the subject that was written back in 1951. The author's name was John S. Arant.

What Mr. Arant had to say is this "For lack of a better name, I have called this *The Triangle of Triumph* and therefore, consistent with the name, since most of these conclusions are built on the geometric figure of the triangle." He continued "All Life and all lives are seated in, and circumscribed by, the triangle. The Author and Source and Director of all life is Himself triune in character – Father, Son, and Holy Spirit. Man is of triple nature – body, mind, and spirit – and within those three there are many triangles – desires, development, decay; intellect, will, sensibilities. Of this "paced interlude in the midst of eternity" which we call time there is the triangle of Past, Present, and Future. Space – that limitless and measureless element of the physical universe – is best known in terms of Height, Breadth, and Depth. Try building yourself some triangles along the lines of your Will, your Work, your Way – You will find some interesting angles.

So, for the first time, I realized that life is designed in a mechanical way to come in threes. That means you don't have to rely on wishing and hoping things turn out okay. You can actually look at the three parts that a particular thing is made of and then apply them to get what you're wanting. Like a three-ingredient recipe or a combination lock. With a combination lock, you need the three exact numbers to unlock the lock...otherwise you will continue to struggle.

Some 40 years later, I accumulated things that work in threes and that's when I knew I needed to share this with anyone wanting answers. To have success/harmony in your life, just apply the three parts of an area you're working on, and things will fall into place. I also learned that the recipe for success with just about anything is by doing these three things, consistently – THINK positively, SPEAK positively and ACT positively. For example, if I want to be a successful artist. I would think to myself "I can do this because I have the talent." Then I would speak it this way "Yes, I am working on my art degree and plan to do portraits professionally." Finally, I would act on that by taking art classes and continue crafting my skill. Eventually, I will see the positive results/success I'm looking for.

Conversely, if I think positively but speak negatively...it will cancel out. Or if I speak positively but have no positive action going on...nothing will happen.

I looked up "How Life Works" and "The Mechanics of Life" and these are really talking about the biology of how our cells work and other chemistry. TRYUNE WORKS! teaches that life is kind of like building blocks. Pick a topic you may be struggling with. See the three parts that topic consists of and then start applying them...on a consistent basis. That will help you overcome the struggle and get you back in harmony/success with how life works.

For 30+ years I was a golf instructor (by accident). My two kids had some success playing junior golf and so friends and neighbors would ask me to show them and their kids how to play golf successfully. From all of this, I got pretty good at watching golfers on the driving range and could spot right away why they were struggling with hitting bad golf shots. I was able to do that because I knew the three steps to hitting good golf shots. I learned them from studying golf and played for several decades. I "broke the code" for me so to speak.

So now you know that life works in threes. You can live your life *by choice* rather than *by chance* and that my friend... is the key to a fulfilling life.

LIFE WORKS
IN THREES!

My sanctuary on the Pacific coast

Introduction

Happiness is like a secret recipe we're all trying to perfect, isn't it? Imagine it as a delicious stew simmering on a stove, made up of all sorts of ingredients: love, laughter, purpose, and maybe even a sprinkle of adventure. But here's the kicker – everyone's recipe is a bit different! What might make your heart do a little dance could be completely different from what gets someone else's spirits soaring. That's what makes understanding happiness such a fascinating journey!

Think of happiness like a cozy blanket on a chilly day – it's comforting, warming, and oh-so-inviting. But here's the conundrum: that blanket isn't one-size-fits-all. Some folks might find their happiness snuggled up with loved ones, while others might discover it in pursuing their passions or simply savoring the small joys of everyday life, like a warm cup of tea or a good book. It's all about finding what makes your heart sing and embracing it with open arms.

Picture this: happiness is like a puzzle, and each of us holds a unique piece. When we come together and share our experiences, we start to see the bigger picture of what happiness truly means. It's not just about chasing after some elusive state of mind; it's about savoring the moments, connecting with others, and finding contentment in the journey itself. So, whether you're basking in the glow of a sunset or sharing a laugh with a friend, remember that happiness is wherever you find it – and it's yours for the taking!

My discovery of the Tryune concept

Before we dive into happiness struggles and how to overcome them, let me share my discovery of the Tryune Concept and how life works in threes. It all began in the summer of 1982.

I grew up with parents who treated everyone with decency and respect. My three older sisters and I were raised in a home that was "middle-class traditional." We lived in modest homes in different small towns, attended school and church on a regular basis and celebrated all the traditional holidays. Eventually we settled during the spring of 1964 in the big city of Houston, Texas. I'll never forget the vastness of the city and hearing sirens from police cars, fire trucks and ambulances on a regular basis. I was excited and scared at the same time.

Once settled in this fast-paced city, I finished my growing-up years with an academic diploma and sweetheart intact. I got a job, bought a car, got married, bought a house and produced two beautiful babies in a span of about 5 years. Talk about having to grow up fast!

Things went from great in my childhood to absolute misery in my young adulthood. I began to struggle with my job because deep down I just hated what I was doing. This problem created a snowball effect because soon after, my weight, my finances, my relationships, my happiness and everything else worth saving was going down the drain. I eventually hit a level of frustration that I had never experienced before and didn't know how to get out of it. My cry for help was for anyone or anything to come to my rescue. I just ran out of solutions for my situation.

This is when my discovery happened.

One night shortly after my meltdown, while sleeping soundly, the word "triune" began to softly pound in my head like a mantra. I woke up a little startled and decided to go look up the word in my favorite dictionary (this was WAY before Google.) The definition said '**triune** (try-une) – 1) a group of three things; united. 2) Being 3 in 1 such as *humans are mental, physical and spiritual.* I scratched my head, got a glass of water and went back to bed.

The next day while driving around town, I began thinking about things that I was taught in my younger years that came in threes. My Boy Scout manual taught that to have **character**, I needed to be *1) physically strong,* 2) *mentally awake and 3) morally straight.* My high school football coach would say emphatically "If you want to be **a good football player**, you have to be *1) mobile 2) agile and 3) hostile!*" My first sales manager shared with me that to be **a successful salesman**, I needed to have *1) sales skills, 2) product knowledge and 3) a good image.*

"Hmm", I thought, "wonder if there are other examples out there of things that work in threes?" So, some 40 years later, I have researched and discovered that many, many things work in threes. What this message was telling me is that to achieve success or balance in any significant area of my life, the three things that area consisted of had to be present continuously. That's when I had my epiphany. This discovery was telling me the secret to how life <u>really</u> works.

Tryune is a play on the word "triune" as an invitation to "try" this concept. Furthermore, we do not say that life <u>only</u> works in threes. Life also works in ones, twos, fours and so on. What has been observed though is that the many things significant to life, just so happen to come and work in threes. That's what is being shared in this book.

Now, you are about to see 40+ years of research and proof that life works in threes. I did not make up any of these topics. I invite you to research them on the internet, as I did, to validate what is written here. There are some interesting facts that most of us have never realized...until now.

How Life Works in Threes (around 200 examples)

<u>LIFE</u>

Humans consist of *body, mind and soul.*

A human's basic needs are *health, income and provisions.*

A human's basic wants are *comfort, gain and approval.*

Our minds are made up of the *conscious, the subconscious and the unconscious.*

Philosophy explains *the id, the ego and superego.*

Atoms consist of *protons, neutrons and electrons.*

Motion is explained by *three basic laws.*

Science falls under three main branches: *natural, social and formal sciences*

Time is *past, present and future*...at the same time.

Electricity consists of *ohms, amperes and voltage.*

Music's basic elements are *duration, pitch and timbre.*

Democracy is a government *of the people, by the people and for the people.*

U.S. branches of government are *the judicial, the executive and the legislative.*

Armed Forces protect us on *land, air and sea.*

Environmentally, we are asked *to reduce, recycle and re-use.*

The news program gives us *the news, sports and conditions.*

Our days consist of *morning, afternoon and evening.*

Three months in each season of the year

Our main meals are known as *breakfast, lunch and dinner.*

A balanced diet consists of *good proteins, carbohydrates and fats.*

Traditional Family consists of *father, mother, and child(ren)*

<u>SCIENCES</u>

Three major branches of natural science – *(physical, earth/space and life sciences)*

Three major branches of modern physics - *(classical, relativistic, quantum)*

Three major branches of biology *(botany, zoology, microbiology)*

Three spatial dimensions: *height* (up/down), *width* (left/right) and *depth* (forwards/backwards)

Three-gauge bosons (photon, gluon, W&Z bosons)

Three types of elementary particles *(leptons, quarks, gauge bosons)*

Three quarks in every proton *(two "up" and one "down")*

Three primary colors of light *(red, green, blue)*

Three color tone properties *(hue, value, chroma)*

Three laws of motion (*Newton's laws*)

Three laws of planetary motion (*Kepler's laws*)

Three layers of the Sun's interior (*core, radiative zone, convective zone*)

Three layers of the Sun's atmosphere (*photosphere, chromosphere, corona*)

Three types of meteorites (*iron, stony iron, stony*)

Three types of galaxy shapes (*elliptical, spiral, irregular*)

Three substances of the universe (*normal matter, 'dark matter', 'dark energy'*)

Three phases of the moon (*new moon, first quarter, full moon*)

Three planetary regions (*temperate, sub-tropical, tropical*)

Three layers of the Earth (*crust, mantle, core*)

Three components of an ecosystem (*producers, consumers, decomposers*)

Three types of rocks (*igneous, sedimentary, metamorphic*)

Three types of fossil fuels (*coal, crude oil, natural gas*)

Three hydrological processes (*evaporation, condensation, precipitation*)

Three basic types of (meteorological) precipitation (*liquid, freezing, frozen*)

Three types of substances *(mono-constituent, multi-constituent, UVCB)*

Three phases of (normal) matter *(solid, liquid, gas)*

Three types of covalent chemical bonds *(single, double and triple bonds)*

Three isotopes of hydrogen *(protium, deuterium, tritium)*

Three atoms in each molecule of water *(two hydrogen atoms and an oxygen atom)*

Three endings to salts *(-ide, -ite, -ate)*

Three requirements for fire *(fuel, oxygen, heat)*

Three nucleotide bases in a genetic codon

Three domains of life *(archaea, bacteria and eukaryotes)*

Three major groups of flowering plants *(monocots, eudicots, magnolids)*

Three major functions that are basic to plant growth and development: *(photosynthesis* [making sugars], *respiration* [metabolizing those sugars], and *transpiration* [water vapor loss]

Three things that the chlorophyll in plants needs for photosynthesis to take place: *(sunlight, carbon dioxide and water)*

Transpiration serves three roles: *(cooling the plant, moving minerals* and *sugars through the plant,* and *maintaining the turgidity pressure* [stiffness] *of the plant's cells)*

Three parts of an insect's body *(head, thorax, abdomen)*

BIOLOGY

Three types of cones in the retina, relating to the three primary colors

Three semi-circular canals in the ear *(lateral, anterior, posterior)*

Three sections in the ear *(outer, middle, inner)*

Three ossicles in the middle ear *(malleus, incus, stapes)*

Three segments to each limb *(proximal, mid, distal)*

Three bones in each arm *(humerus, radius, ulna)*

Three joints in the arm *(shoulder, elbow, wrist)*

Three joints in the leg *(hip, knee, ankle)*

Three joints in the elbow *(humeroulnar, humeroradial, proximal radioulnar)*

Three functional compartments in the knee joint *(the femoropatellar, medial femorotibial* and *lateral femorotibial articulations)*

Three types of fibrous joints *(sutures, gomphoses, syndesmoses)*

Three types of bone in each hand (*carpals, metacarpals, phalanges*)

Three types of bone in each foot (*tarsals, metatarsals, phalanges*)

Three bones (phalanges) in each finger and in each toe (*proximal, intermediate, distal*)

Three layers of skin (*dermis, epidermis, hypodermis*)

Three components of a cell (*cell membrane, nucleus, cytoplasm*)

Three types of blood vessels (*arteries, veins, capillaries*)

Three types of blood cells [*red* (erythrocytes), *white* (leukocytes), *platelets* (thrombocytes)]

Three processes of the intestinal tract (*ingestion, digestion, excretion*)

Three germ layers (*Endoderm, Mesoderm, Ectoderm*)

Three parts of a human tooth (*crown, neck, root*)

Three organs of otolaryngology (*ear, nose, throat*)

Three major body systems (*digestive, circulatory, respiratory*)

Three parts to a neuron: (*soma* [*cell body*], *axon, dendrites*)

Three main parts of the brain (*forebrain, midbrain, hindbrain*)

Three parts of the forebrain (*cerebrum, thalamus, hypothalamus*)

Three parts of the midbrain (*colliculi, tegmentum, cerebral peduncles*)

Three parts of the hindbrain (*cerebellum, pons, medulla*)

Three membranes enclosing the brain (*dura mater, arachnoid, pia mater*)

The brain operates on three levels: *consciously* (for cognitive thought and declarative memory); *subconsciously* (for pre-planned actions and procedural memory); and *unconsciously* (for breathing, heart beating, etc.)

Our conscious mind is fed from three sources: *our senses* (which can be fooled); *our memory* (which is flawed); and *our imagination* (which is inventive)

Three aspects of the human mind (*memory, intellect, will*)

Three parts of the human personality (*id, ego, superego*)

The sum of human capacity consists of three abilities (*thought, word and deed*)

Three times of man (*birth, life, death*)

Three periods of the Gait Cycle (*initial double limb support, single limb support, and terminal double limb support*)

MUSIC

Three types of musical notes (*sharps, flats, naturals*)

Three aspects of a song (*lyrics, melody, rhythm*)

Three types of musical chords (*root, third, fifth*)

MATHEMATICS

Three types of a real number (*positive, negative, zero*)

Three parts to any arithmetic operation: for addition: *augend, addend and sum* - for subtraction: *minuend, subtrahend and difference* - for multiplication: *multiplicand, multiplier and product* - for division: *dividend, divisor and quotient*

Three laws of arithmetic operations (*commutative, associative, distributive*)

Three types of equivalence relation (*reflexivity, symmetry, transitivity*)

Three types of symmetry operations (*translation, rotation, reflection*)

Three geometries (*Euclidean, spherical, hyperbolic*)

The number 3 is the basis of an entire branch of mathematics, called trigonometry (from the Greek *trigonon* "triangle" + *metron* "measure")

Three trigonometric functions (*sine, cosine, tangent*)

Three types of average (*mean, mode, median*)

GRAMMAR

Three logical operators (*AND, OR and NOT*)

Three laws of logic (*identity, noncontradiction, excluded middle*)

Three parts of a logical syllogism (*major premise, minor premise, conclusion*)

Three grammatical parts to a sentence (*subject, verb, complement*)

Three persons in grammar [*1st person* (I/we), *2nd* (you or your), *3rd* (he/she/it/they)]

Three genders in grammar [*masculine* (he/him), *feminine* (she/her), *neuter* (it)]

Three forms of comparison in grammar [*positive, comparative* (more, -er), *superlative* (most, -est)]

Three cases in (English) grammar [*subjective/nominative* (he), *objective/accusative* (him) and *possessive/genitive* (his)]

Three parts of a narrative (*beginning, middle, end*)

Components of an essay (*introduction, body, conclusion*)

Elements of a rhetorical appeal (*ethos, pathos, logos*)

Aspects of a story (*plot, characters, setting*)

<u>RELIGION</u>

The Creator – *omniscient, omnipotent, omnipresent*

Christian God – *Father, Son, Holy Spirit*

Jesus – *The Way, The Truth, The Life*

Ancient Near East- *Qudshu, Astarte, Anat*

Classical Antiquity – Many dieties came in threes

Hinduism – Para Brahman is *Brahma, Visnu, Shiva*

Ancient Celtic Cultures – *many example of triad dieties*

Buddhism – *The three jewels*

Taoism – *The three pure ones*

Islam – *Fear, Hope and Love*

Baha'i - *Intention, Power and Action*

Confucianism – *Benevolence, Wisdom and Courage*

<u>OTHER TRIUNE EXAMPLES</u>

3 Coins in a Fountain

3 Days of the Condor

3 Miles in a League

3 Goals in a Hat Trick

3 Piece Suit

3 Feet in a Yard

3 Books in Lord of the Rings

3 Ring Circus

3 Ships of Christopher Columbus

3 Sheets to the Wind

3 Books in a Trilogy

3 Wheels on a Tricycle

3 Wise Men

3-Legged Race

3 Ring Circus

3-Wheeler

3 Cornered Hat

3 Dimensional

3 Musketeers

3 R's (reading, 'riting, 'rithmatic)

3 Sides of a triangle

3 Races in the Triple Crown (horse racing)

3 Angles in a Triangle

3 Trimesters in a Pregnancy

3 Flavors in Neapolitan Ice Cream

3 Stars in Orion's belt

3 Barleycorns in an Inch

3 Hands on a Clock (with the Seconds Hand)

3 Colors in a Flag

3 Minute Egg

3 Great Pyramids at Giza

3 Holes in a Bowling Ball

3 Colors in a Set of Traffic Lights

3 Minutes in a Boxing Round

3 Teaspoons in a Tablespoon

3 Legs on a Stool

3 Monastic Vows (Obience, Stability, Conversatio Morum)

3 Body Types: Endomorph, Mesomorph, Ectomorph

3 Ring Notebooks

3 Germ layers: Endoderm, Mesoderm, Ectoderm

3 Species of Homo: Homo habilis, Homo erectus, Homo sapiens

3 Basic parts of a camera: Lens, Shutter, Sensor

3 Stages of a Project lifecycle: initiation, planning, execution

The Truth, The Whole Truth and Nothing but the Truth

Life, Liberty and the Pursuit of Happiness

Hear no Evil, See no Evil, Speak no Evil

National motto of France/Haiti: Liberty, Equality, Fraternity

Paper, Rock, Scissors

Ready, Aim, Fire

On Your mark, Get Set, Go

Olympic medals of gold, silver, bronze

Types of joints (ball & socket, hinge, pivot)

Stages of a rocket launch (launch, orbit, re-entry)

Parts of a joke (setup, delivery, punchline)

Primary components of a transistor (emitter, base, collector)

Primary components of an airplane (fuselage, wings, empennage)

Basic components of a computer: CPU, memory, storage

Three phases in the development of technology (*eotechnic* [*mechanical*], *paleotechnic* [*steam-powered*] and *neotechnic* [*electric-powered*]

Communication systems require three components (*transmitter, channel, receiver*)

The list goes on. See if you can find more examples as they are everywhere in our universe! Now that you know that life works in threes (with proof!), we can begin to apply this concept to whatever topics we want.

So, to overcome struggles with happiness*, we need to apply the three areas that happiness consists of – MINDSET, ENVIRONMENT and EXPECTATIONS. Let's get started!

When dealing with topics such as happiness, it is important to note that there are **mild, moderate and **extreme** cases of unhappiness. If you feel that you may be in the moderate to extreme category, it may behoove you to seek counsel from a mental health professional. TRYUNE WORKS! is not a clinically certified organization offering medical advice. We are simply sharing research that was developed while exploring the keys to happiness.*

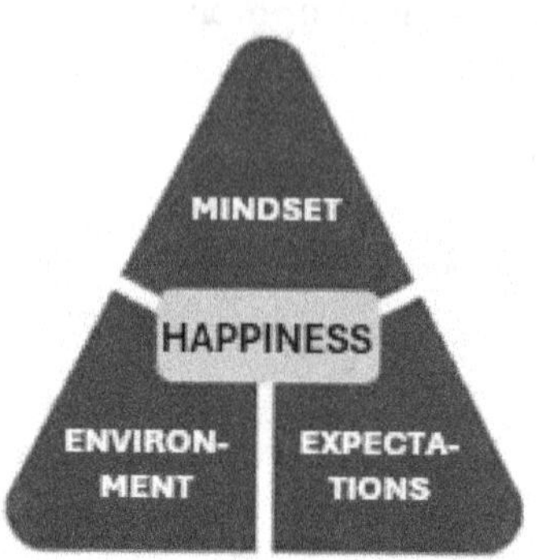

MINDSET
HAPPINESS
ENVIRON-
MENT
EXPECTA-
TIONS

HAPPINESS

Happiness is that warm feeling you get when everything just clicks into place, like finding the last piece of a puzzle or catching up with an old friend over coffee. It's not about having a permanent smile plastered on your face or being in a constant state of euphoria. Instead, it's those moments of contentment and fulfillment that make life feel meaningful and worthwhile.

Contrary to what some might think, happiness isn't about avoiding negative emotions altogether. It's okay to feel sad, frustrated, or even angry at times; these emotions are part of being human. Happiness is more about how you bounce back from those lows, finding resilience and strength in the face of challenges. It's about embracing the full spectrum of emotions and learning from them, rather than pretending they don't exist by living in denial.

Finally, happiness isn't something you can buy off the shelf or achieve through external achievements alone. While achieving goals or acquiring material possessions can bring temporary satisfaction, true happiness often lies in the simpler things: connecting with loved ones, pursuing passions, or simply enjoying a quiet moment of solitude. It's about cultivating meaningful relationships, pursuing personal growth, and finding a sense of purpose that resonates with your values and beliefs. Ultimately, happiness is a journey, not a destination, and it's different for everyone. It's about discovering what truly fulfills you and brings you joy in your own unique way.

In a nutshell, if you want to be happy...move from judgement to gratitude. This has been quoted by several sources and really hit home for me when I first heard it. With age, gratitude gets easier I found out.

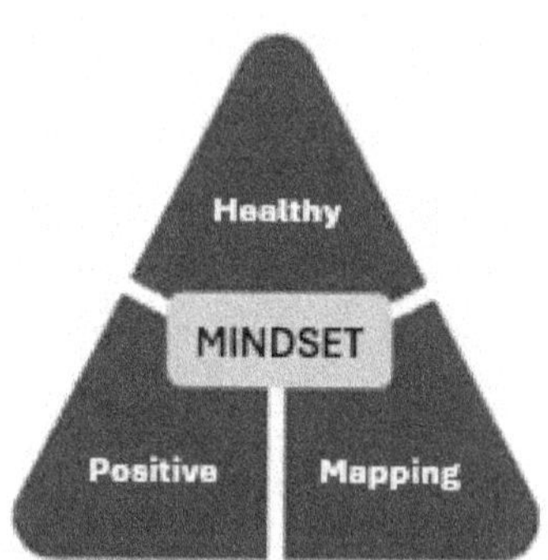

Healthy
MINDSET
Positive
Mapping

MINDSET

Alright, let's break it down like this: imagine your mindset is like the captain of your mental ship, steering you through the choppy waters of life. It's not just about what happens to you, but how you perceive and react to it. Your mindset is the lens through which you view the world, shaping your thoughts, beliefs, and actions. Think of it as your very own superpower, influencing everything from how you tackle challenges to how you embrace opportunities.

Now, here's the fun part: your mindset isn't set in stone! It's more like a garden that you tend to, nurturing it with positivity, resilience, and a dash of self-belief. You see, the beauty of mindset is that it's malleable – you have the power to cultivate a mindset that serves you best. Whether you're facing setbacks or soaring to new heights, your mindset is there, cheering you on like a trusty sidekick.

So, what does all this mean in the grand scheme of things? Well, it's simple: mindset is the magic ingredient that can turn obstacles into steppingstones and dreams into reality. It's about embracing the power of "yet" – recognizing that even if you haven't reached your goals *yet*, with the right mindset, anything is possible. So, let your mindset be your compass, guiding you towards a life filled with growth, resilience, and endless possibilities.

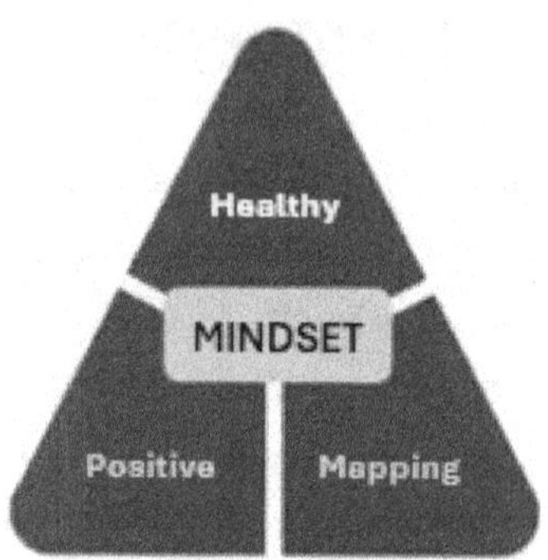
Healthy
MINDSET
Positive
Mapping

Healthy

Let's take a gentle stroll through the garden of mental wellbeing, where the sun shines bright and the air is filled with the scent of positivity. Just like tending to a delicate flower, keeping our minds healthy requires nurturing and care. One way we can do this is by steering clear of mind-altering substances that can cloud our judgment and dim the brightness of our inner light.

Think of your mind as a pristine lake, reflecting the beauty of the world around you. When we introduce mind-altering substances into the mix, it's like tossing a stone into that serene lake, disrupting the calm and distorting the reflection. Whether it's alcohol, drugs, or other substances, they can create ripples of chaos in our minds, leaving us feeling lost and disconnected from ourselves and others.

Instead of relying on external substances to cope with life's challenges, let's cultivate healthy coping mechanisms that nourish our minds and souls. Whether it's spending time in nature, practicing mindfulness and meditation, or connecting with loved ones, there are countless ways to find solace and peace without resorting to mind-altering substances. By embracing these healthy habits, we not only protect our mental wellbeing but also deepen our connection to ourselves and the world around us. So, let's choose to keep our minds clear and our spirits bright, embracing the beauty of sobriety and the endless possibilities it brings.

I also recommend visiting a mental coach/therapist if necessary. One of the best things I ever did was receive advice from a dear friend who knew what I was going through. After several sessions with my therapist, I came away with helpful tools to get me through my tough time and come back to normal. Big help!

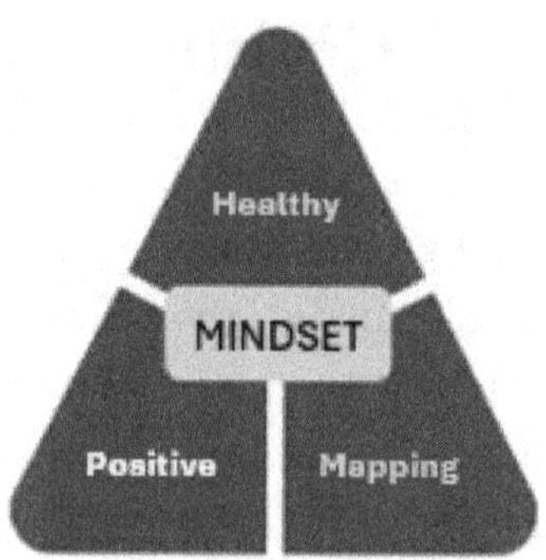
Healthy
MINDSET
Positive
Mapping

Positive

Let's embark on a journey to explore the colorful landscapes of attitude, where the contrast between positivity and negativity paints a vivid picture of how we perceive the world around us. Picture it like two paths diverging in a lush forest – one bathed in sunlight and filled with chirping birds, while the other is shrouded in darkness with ominous whispers in the air. The choice between a positive and negative attitude isn't just about what happens to us, but how we choose to respond to life's twists and turns.

First off, let's talk about **positivity** – it's like a ray of sunshine on a cloudy day, brightening everything it touches. When you approach life with a positive attitude, challenges become opportunities, setbacks become steppingstones, and even the darkest of days hold a glimmer of hope. It's like wearing a pair of magical glasses that filter out negativity and highlight the beauty and joy that surrounds us, even in the most unexpected places.

Now, let's wander down the path of **negativity** – it's like trudging through mud with lead weights strapped to your feet. When you approach life with a negative attitude, even the smallest setbacks can feel like insurmountable obstacles, and every disappointment becomes confirmation of your worst fears. It's like viewing the world through a cracked lens, where everything appears distorted and bleak, and even the brightest moments are overshadowed by a sense of impending doom.

So, which path will you choose? Will you embrace the sunshine of positivity, filling your days with warmth and possibility? Or will you linger in the shadows of negativity, weighed down by doubt and despair? Remember, the choice is yours, and each step you take shapes the landscape of your journey. So, let your attitude be a compass guiding you towards a brighter, happier tomorrow, where every moment is filled with potential and promise.

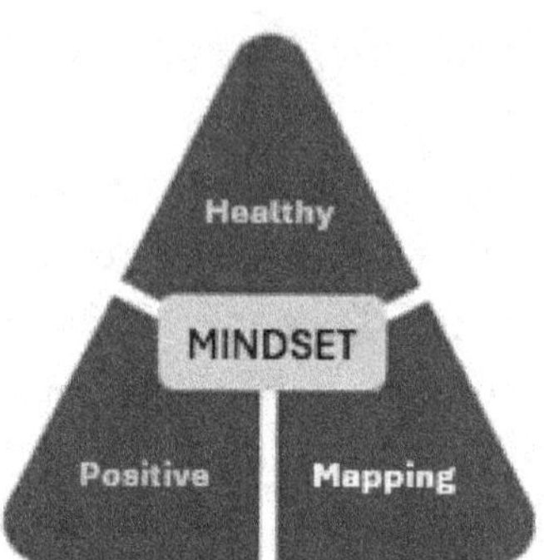
Healthy
MINDSET
Positive
Mapping

Mapping

Alright, let's dive into the colorful world of mind mapping – it's like creating a treasure map for your thoughts and ideas! Picture it like doodling with a purpose, where every squiggle and doodad represents a new avenue of exploration. Mind mapping isn't just about organizing information; it's about unleashing your creativity and tapping into the boundless potential of your mind.

First off, let's talk about **brainstorming** – it's like tossing a handful of seeds into fertile soil and watching them sprout into vibrant ideas. Mind mapping is like giving your brainstorming sessions a turbo boost, allowing your thoughts to flow freely and organically without the constraints of linear thinking. Whether you're planning a project, solving a problem, or simply jotting down your thoughts, mind mapping helps you visualize connections and uncover hidden insights in a way that feels playful and intuitive.

Next up, let's sprinkle in a dash of **organization** – it's like tidying up your mental clutter and creating a roadmap for success. With mind mapping, you can break down complex concepts into bite-sized chunks, arranging them in a way that makes sense to you. It's like putting together a puzzle, where each piece fits seamlessly into the bigger picture, guiding you towards your goals with clarity and purpose.

Last but not least, let's talk about **memory** – it's like flexing a muscle that grows stronger with exercise. Studies have shown that mind mapping can improve retention and recall by engaging both hemispheres of the brain in a dynamic dance of creativity and logic. So, whether you're studying for an exam, preparing for a presentation, or simply trying to remember where you left your keys, mind mapping can be a powerful tool for harnessing the full potential of your mind. So, grab your pens and paper, and let your imagination run wild – the world is your canvas, and your mind map is the masterpiece in the making!

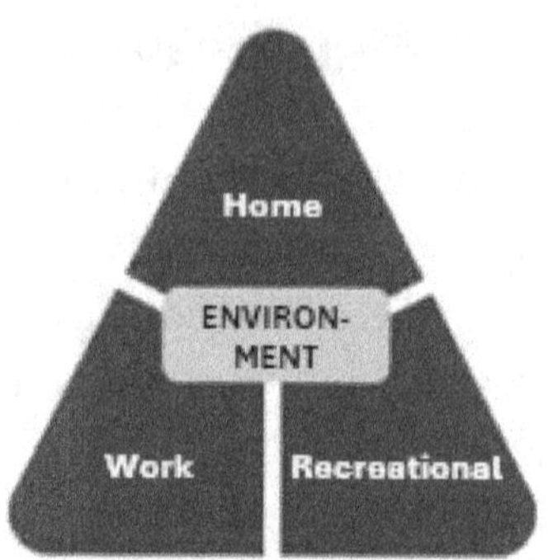

Home
ENVIRON-
MENT
Work
Recreational

ENVIRONMENT

Imagine your environment as the stage where the grand play of life unfolds – it sets the scene, shapes the mood, and influences the characters' actions. From the cozy warmth of your home to the bustling energy of a crowded street, every nook and cranny of our surroundings has a story to tell and an impact on our behavior. Let's take a leisurely stroll through the intricate dance of environment and behavior, shall we?

Let's look at the power of **context** – it's like the invisible hand guiding our actions and decisions. Have you ever noticed how your behavior shifts depending on where you are and who you're with? That's the magic of environment at work! Whether you're at work, at home, or out with friends, your environment sets the stage for how you interact with the world around you. It's like slipping into different costumes for different scenes of the play, adapting your behavior to fit the role you're playing in that moment.

Then we'll sprinkle in a dash of **social influence** – it's like a ripple effect that spreads through the fabric of our environment. Humans are social creatures by nature, and we're constantly influenced by the people around us. Whether it's the cheerful laughter of friends lifting your spirits or the tense atmosphere of a heated argument making you feel on edge, our behavior is deeply intertwined with the social dynamics of our environment. By surrounding ourselves with positive influences and supportive relationships, we can create a nurturing environment that fosters growth and wellbeing.

Finally, let's talk about the power of **design** – it's like the secret sauce that shapes our experiences and perceptions. From the layout of a room to the colors on the walls, the design of our environment can have a profound impact on our behavior and mood. Just think about how walking into a bright, airy space can lift your spirits, or how being surrounded by clutter can make you feel overwhelmed and stressed. By intentionally designing our environments to support our goals and values, we can create spaces that inspire creativity, foster connection, and nourish our souls. So, whether you're sprucing up your home or redesigning your workspace, remember that your environment has the power to shape your behavior and transform your life.

Let me just say that it is next to impossible to "fix" people. When you live, work or play with dysfunctional people, the chances of them changing to your way of thinking or behaving are slim to none. If you get to a point where you can't tolerate a toxic person or work environment, the healthy thing to do, in all honesty, is to <u>remove yourself from there.</u> There are healthy people and work environments at other places. Seek them out so you can get back to peace of mind and thrive in your environments of home, work and play.

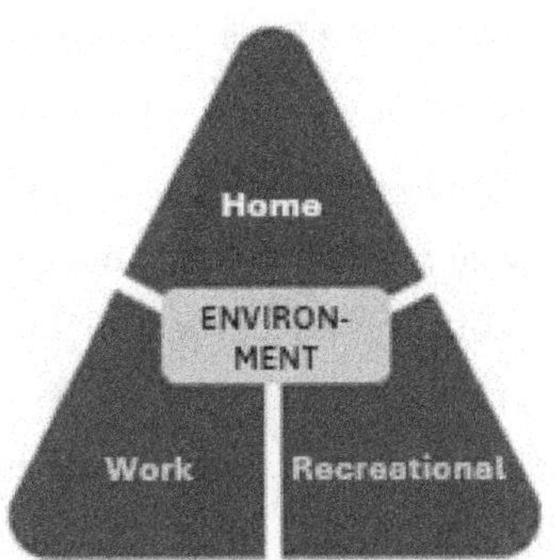
Home
ENVIRON-
MENT
Work
Recreational

Home

Let's take a peek into the cozy world of home life, where the vibes can range from warm and welcoming to, well, not so much. Picture it like two sides of the same coin – one bathed in sunshine and filled with laughter, while the other is shrouded in shadows with an air of tension. The differences between a healthy and unhealthy home life can have a profound impact on our wellbeing, shaping our experiences and perceptions in ways both big and small.

Importantly, we have **communication** – it's like the glue that holds relationships together. In a healthy home life, communication flows freely like a babbling brook, with family members sharing their thoughts, feelings, and concerns openly and honestly. It's about listening with empathy, expressing yourself respectfully, and working together to find solutions to any challenges that arise. *On the flip side, in an unhealthy home life, communication can feel more like a game of telephone gone wrong, with misunderstandings piling up like tangled spaghetti. Whether it's avoiding difficult conversations or resorting to passive-aggressive behavior, poor communication can create a breeding ground for resentment and conflict.*

The next important ingredient is **boundaries** – it's like drawing lines in the sand to protect your peace of mind. In a healthy home life, boundaries are like sturdy fences, establishing clear guidelines for behavior and ensuring that everyone's needs are respected. It's about striking a balance between independence and interdependence, allowing each family member to express themselves authentically while also being mindful of how their actions impact others. *In an unhealthy home life, boundaries can feel more like flimsy picket fences, easily trampled over by the whims and desires of others. Whether it's overstepping personal space or disregarding individual preferences, a lack of boundaries can lead to feelings of resentment, frustration, and burnout.*

And of course, let's talk about **support** – it's like having a safety net to catch you when you fall. In a healthy home life, support is like a warm hug on a cold day, with family members rallying around each other during both the good times and the bad. It's about being there for one another, offering a listening ear, a shoulder to cry on, or a helping hand whenever it's needed. *On the flip side, in an unhealthy home life, support can feel more like a scarce resource, with family members either too caught up in their own struggles to offer help or actively undermining each other's efforts to grow and thrive. Whether it's fostering a sense of belonging or providing emotional validation, a lack of support can leave us feeling isolated and disconnected from those we love most.*

So, whether your home life is a sanctuary of love and laughter or a battleground of tension and turmoil, remember that you have the power to shape your environment and create the nurturing, supportive space you deserve.

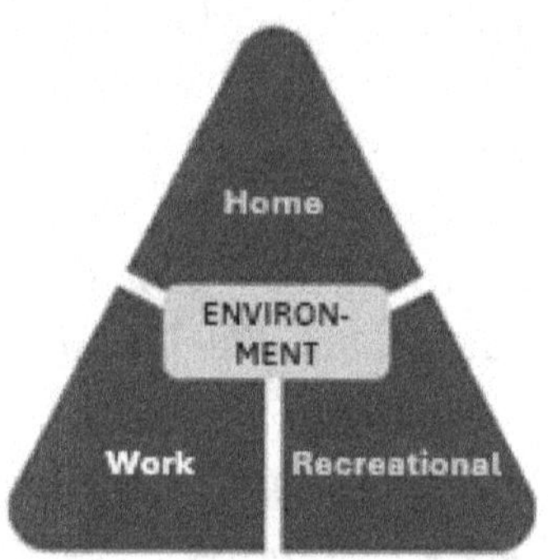

Home
ENVIRON-
MENT
Work
Recreational

Work

Let's step into the bustling world of work environments, where the vibes can range from energizing and uplifting to, well, a bit of a slog. Picture it like two different office parties – one filled with high-fives and team spirit, while the other feels more like a scene from "Office Space." The differences between a healthy and unhealthy work environment can make all the difference in how we feel about our jobs and ourselves.

Work communication – it's like the engine that keeps the workplace humming along smoothly. In a healthy work environment, communication flows freely like a well-oiled machine, with colleagues sharing ideas, feedback, and concerns in an open and respectful manner. It's about fostering a culture of transparency and collaboration, where everyone feels valued and heard. *On the flip side, in an unhealthy work environment, communication can feel more like a game of telephone gone wrong, with messages getting lost in translation and tensions simmering beneath the surface. Whether it's micromanaging bosses or passive-aggressive coworkers, poor communication can create a toxic atmosphere that stifles creativity and innovation.*

Work support – it's like having a safety net to catch you when you stumble. In a healthy work environment, support is like a warm cup of coffee on a Monday morning, with colleagues and managers cheering each other on and offering a helping hand when needed. It's about fostering a sense of camaraderie and teamwork, where everyone pitches in to help each other succeed. *On the flip side, in an unhealthy work environment, support can feel more like a scarce resource, with colleagues competing against each other rather than collaborating. Whether it's lackluster training programs or unsupportive management, a lack of support can leave employees feeling overwhelmed and demoralized.*

Work-life balance – it's like finding the perfect harmony between the two. In a healthy work environment, work-life balance is like a well-choreographed dance, with employees feeling empowered to prioritize their personal lives and recharge their batteries outside of the office. It's about recognizing that happy and fulfilled employees are more productive and engaged, and fostering a culture that values both work and play. *On the flip side, in an unhealthy work environment, work-life balance can feel more like a distant dream, with long hours, unrealistic expectations, and constant pressure to perform taking a toll on your mental and physical health.*

Whether it's flexible work schedules or generous vacation policies, prioritizing work-life balance can make all the difference in creating a workplace where you can thrive.

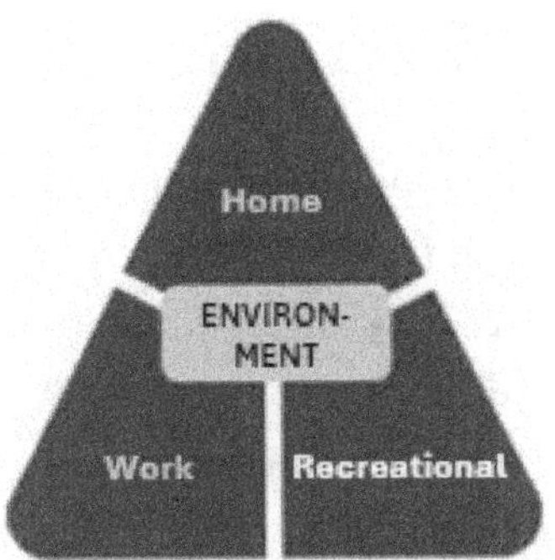
Home
ENVIRON-
MENT
Work
Recreational

Recreational

Let's take a delightful jaunt into the realm of recreational environments, where the vibes can range from invigorating and rejuvenating to, well, a bit of a downer. Picture it like two different weekend getaways – one filled with laughter and adventure, while the other feels more like a staycation gone wrong. The differences between a healthy and unhealthy recreational environment can greatly influence our mood, energy levels, and overall sense of wellbeing.

Activities – it's like the spice that adds flavor to our leisure time. In a healthy recreational environment, activities are like a smorgasbord of options, offering something for everyone to enjoy. Whether it's hiking through scenic trails, dancing the night away with friends, or simply curling up with a good book, the possibilities are endless. It's about finding activities that nourish your body, mind, and soul, leaving you feeling refreshed and rejuvenated. *On the flip side, in an unhealthy recreational environment, activities can feel more like a chore than a source of joy. Whether it's engaging in activities that drain your energy or spending time with people who bring you down, the wrong activities can leave you feeling depleted and uninspired.*

Connection – it's like the secret ingredient that adds depth and richness to our recreational experiences. In a healthy recreational environment, connection is like a warm embrace, with friends and loved ones coming together to share laughter, create memories, and strengthen bonds. It's about fostering meaningful connections with others, whether it's through shared experiences, heartfelt conversations, or acts of kindness. *On the flip side, in an unhealthy recreational environment, connection can feel more like a distant dream, with social interactions that feel forced or superficial. Whether it's spending time with people who drain your energy or feeling disconnected from those around you, a lack of meaningful connections can leave you feeling lonely and isolated.*

Relaxation – it's like pressing the reset button on your mind and body. In a healthy recreational environment, relaxation is like sinking into a warm bubble bath after a long day, with opportunities to unwind and recharge your batteries. Whether it's taking a leisurely stroll through nature, practicing mindfulness and meditation, or indulging in a soothing spa day, relaxation is an essential part of self-care. *On the flip side, in an unhealthy recreational environment, relaxation can feel more like an afterthought than a priority. Whether it's constantly being on the go or feeling overwhelmed by the demands of everyday life, a lack of relaxation can leave you feeling stressed and burnt out.*

So, whether you're planning your next weekend getaway or simply looking for ways to unwind after a busy day, remember to prioritize activities that nourish your body, mind, and soul, leaving you feeling refreshed and revitalized.

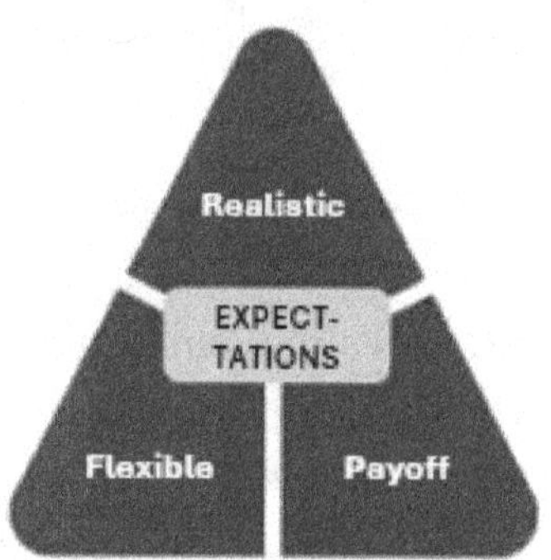

Realistic
EXPECT-
TATIONS
Flexible
Payoff

EXPECTATIONS

Let's explore the realms of expectations, where the balance between reality and fantasy can make all the difference in our happiness and wellbeing. Picture it like two different road trips – one with a clear map and realistic expectations, while the other is guided by wishful thinking and lofty dreams. The differences between realistic and unrealistic expectations can shape our experiences, relationships, and overall satisfaction with life.

Goals – it's like setting the GPS for your journey through life. In a healthy mindset, realistic expectations are like a well-marked trail, guiding you towards achievable goals and milestones. It's about setting yourself up for success by setting goals that are challenging yet attainable, allowing you to celebrate progress and stay motivated along the way. *On the flip side, unrealistic expectations are like chasing after a mirage in the desert, constantly moving further away no matter how fast you run. Whether it's expecting instant success or setting impossibly high standards for yourself, unrealistic expectations can lead to feelings of frustration, disappointment, and burnout.*

Self-compassion – it's like a soothing balm for the soul. In a healthy mindset, realistic expectations are like a warm hug from a friend, allowing you to acknowledge your strengths and weaknesses with kindness and understanding. It's about accepting yourself as you are, imperfections and all, and recognizing that it's okay to stumble along the way. *On the flip side, unrealistic expectations can be like a harsh critic, constantly berating you for not measuring up to impossible standards of perfection. Whether it's beating yourself up over mistakes or constantly comparing yourself to others, unrealistic expectations can erode your self-esteem and rob you of joy and contentment.*

Relationships – it's like navigating the waters of connection with grace and empathy. In a healthy mindset, realistic expectations are like a sturdy ship, weathering the storms of life with resilience and strength. It's about accepting others as they are, flaws and all, and recognizing that no one is perfect. *On the flip side, unrealistic expectations can be like a leaky boat, constantly taking on water and threatening to sink under the weight of unmet demands. Whether it's expecting your partner to fulfill all your needs or believing that your friendships should be free of conflict, unrealistic expectations can strain relationships and create unnecessary tension.*

So, whether you're setting goals, practicing self-compassion, or nurturing your relationships, remember to approach life with realistic expectations and a healthy dose of kindness and understanding.

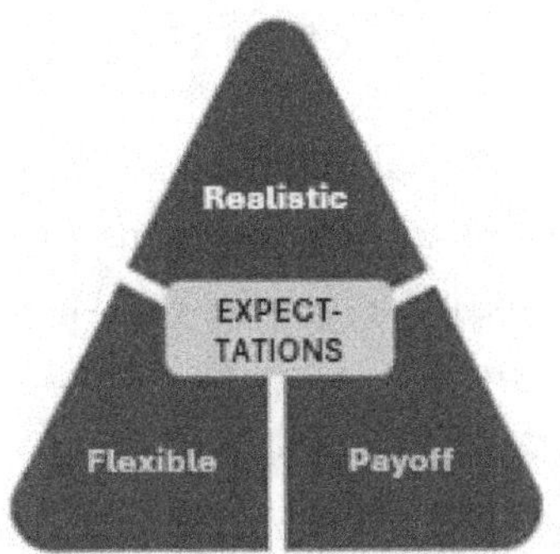
Realistic
EXPECT-
TATIONS
Flexible
Payoff

Realistic

Let's look at a friendly exploration of realistic expectations, shall we? Picture it like packing for a trip – you want to bring just the right amount of luggage without overloading yourself with unnecessary baggage. Realistic expectations are like that perfectly packed suitcase, filled with hopes and dreams that are grounded in the reality of what's achievable.

Goal-setting – it's like planting seeds of possibility in the garden of your life. Realistic expectations are like planting seeds in fertile soil, choosing goals that are challenging yet attainable. It's about setting yourself up for success by breaking big goals down into smaller, more manageable steps. Whether it's aiming to improve your skills at work, nurturing your relationships, or prioritizing self-care, realistic expectations set you on a path of steady progress and growth.

Self-acceptance – it's like giving yourself a warm hug on a chilly day. Realistic expectations are like wrapping yourself in a cozy blanket of understanding and kindness, accepting yourself as you are, imperfections and all. It's about recognizing that it's okay to stumble along the way, and that failure is simply a steppingstone on the path to success. Whether it's acknowledging your strengths, forgiving your mistakes, or being gentle with yourself when things don't go as planned, realistic expectations allow you to navigate life with grace and resilience.

Others – it's like tending to the garden of connection with care and attention. Realistic expectations are like watering your relationships with love and understanding, accepting others as they are, flaws and all. It's about recognizing that no one is perfect, and that every relationship will have its ups and downs. Whether it's communicating openly, setting boundaries, or being patient with each other's quirks, realistic expectations foster deeper connections and greater harmony.

So, whether you're setting goals, practicing self-compassion, or nurturing your relationships with others, remember to approach life with realistic expectations and a friendly dose of kindness and understanding.

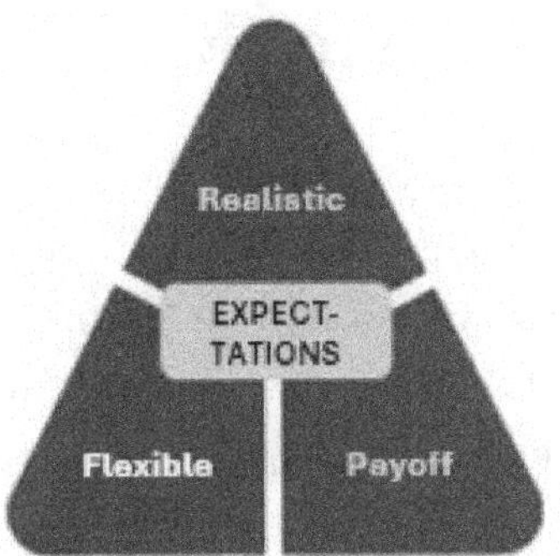
Realistic
EXPECT-
TATIONS
Flexible
Payoff

Flexible

Let's take a delightful stroll through the garden of attitudes, where flexibility and rigidity play key roles in shaping our experiences and interactions with the world around us. Picture it like dancing in the rain – one with graceful movements that flow with the rhythm, while the other feels more like marching in place. The differences between a flexible and rigid attitude can greatly influence how we navigate life's twists and turns.

Adaptability – it's like being a chameleon that blends seamlessly with its surroundings. A flexible attitude is like a sprightly dancer, able to pivot and adjust to changing circumstances with ease and grace. It's about embracing life's uncertainties with an open mind and a willingness to try new things. Whether it's adapting to unexpected challenges, embracing different perspectives, or rolling with the punches when things don't go as planned, a flexible attitude allows you to navigate life's ever-changing landscape with resilience and optimism.

Stamina – it's like bouncing back from setbacks with grace and determination. A flexible attitude is like a sturdy tree that bends but doesn't break in the face of adversity. It's about viewing setbacks as opportunities for growth and learning, rather than roadblocks to success. Whether it's overcoming obstacles at work, navigating conflicts in relationships, or persevering through personal challenges, a flexible attitude allows you to bounce back stronger and more resilient than ever.

Flexible vs rigid – it's like dancing with a partner who knows all the right steps. A flexible attitude is like a graceful partner on the dance floor, able to adapt and respond to the needs of others with empathy and understanding. It's about being open to compromise, listening actively, and finding common ground even when opinions differ. Whether it's resolving conflicts, supporting loved ones through tough times, or building stronger connections with those around you, a flexible attitude fosters harmony and cooperation in relationships.

Dr. Wayne Dyer advocated "having a mind that is open to everything and attached to nothing." While author Ken Keyes, Jr. explained that we should *downgrade our demands to a preference*. Instead of demanding how things <u>must </u>be...just <u>prefer </u>them to be a certain way and if they aren't...then just shake it off.

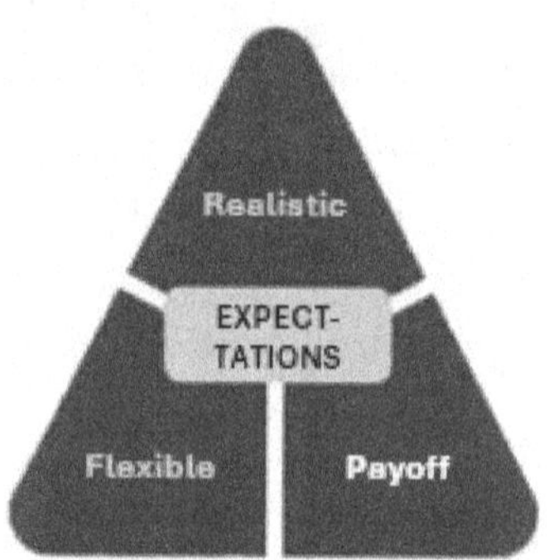
Realistic
EXPECT-
TATIONS
Flexible
Payoff

Payoff

What is the payoff of our actions? It's like uncovering hidden treasures in the vast landscape of life. Picture it like planting seeds in a garden, where every action we take has the potential to bloom into something beautiful. The payoff of our actions isn't always immediate or obvious, but with a little patience and perspective, we can discover the true value of our efforts. We must always ask ourselves "What's in it for me?"

Intention – it's similar to setting the compass for our journey through life. Understanding the payoff of our actions begins with clarifying our intentions and aligning them with our values and goals. It's about asking ourselves why we're doing what we're doing and what we hope to achieve in the long run. Whether it's pursuing a passion, helping others, or striving for personal growth, having a clear sense of purpose guides our actions and gives them meaning beyond the surface level.

Patience – it's likened to waiting for the seeds we've planted to sprout and grow. The payoff of our actions isn't always immediate, and it often requires perseverance and resilience to see things through to fruition. It's about trusting the process and believing that our efforts will eventually pay off, even when progress feels slow or setbacks arise. Whether it's working towards a career goal, building a relationship, or making positive lifestyle changes, patience allows us to stay focused on the bigger picture and maintain faith in our abilities.

Reflection – taking a step back to admire the garden we've cultivated. Understanding the payoff of our actions involves reflecting on our experiences and learning from both our successes and failures. It's about celebrating our achievements, no matter how small, and acknowledging the lessons we've gained along the way. Whether it's recognizing the impact of our actions on others, identifying areas for growth, or simply appreciating how far we've come, reflection deepens our understanding of the payoff of our actions and empowers us to continue striving towards our goals with renewed purpose and enthusiasm.

Healthy
MINDSET
Positive
Mapping
Home
HAPPINESS
Realistic
ENVIRON-
MENT
EXPECT-
ATIONS
Work
Recreational
Flexible
Payoff

SUMMARY

Happiness can be as elusive as a butterfly flitting through a sun-dappled meadow. Picture it like a jigsaw puzzle, with each piece representing a different aspect of what happiness is – and isn't. The quest to understand happiness is like piecing together this puzzle, discovering that it's not just a destination but a journey filled with twists, turns, and unexpected surprises.

What happiness isn't – it's not a constant state of euphoria or a never-ending stream of positive emotions. Happiness isn't about plastering a smile on your face and pretending that everything is sunshine and rainbows all the time. It's not about chasing after fleeting pleasures or external validations, hoping that they'll fill the void and bring lasting fulfillment.

What happiness is – it's like finding contentment and peace in the present moment, regardless of external circumstances. Happiness is about embracing life with open arms, celebrating the highs and weathering the lows with grace and resilience. It's about nurturing meaningful connections with others, finding purpose and meaning in our pursuits, and savoring the small joys that make life worth living.

Perspective – it's like adjusting the lens through which we view the world. Understanding what happiness is and isn't involves shifting our perspective from seeking happiness as an end goal to embracing it as a byproduct of living authentically and intentionally. It's about letting go of unrealistic expectations and embracing life's imperfections with a sense of humor and humility.

Invitation

What I want to suggest here, if you haven't already done it, is to make a deal with yourself. Instead of telling yourself "I won't be happy until I have what I want." For example: "I won't be happy until I have that designer purse." or "I won't be happy until I'm earning one million dollars per year." or "I won't be happy until my children start making straight As in school." and so on.

Instead, let's decide to be happy, no matter what is going on in our lives and have preferences. For example: "I'm looking forward to earning more money but in the meantime, I will continue to budget wisely." or "I'm so lucky to have healthy kids and will continue to work with them on achieving more." You get the picture.

When we make "demands" on how things MUST be, we set ourselves up for disappointments. By switching to "preferring" how things could be, the pressure is off. We are imperfect people living in an imperfect world. So, expecting perfection is generally the cause of unhappiness. We can treat the cause, rather than the symptoms, by preferring how we would like things to be.

Over the years I battled with the meaning of life or the purpose of life and came to the conclusion that the correct question to ask is: "What is life about?" Here's my take on it.

1. Life is about going after what you need and want. You can't have what you want until you get what you need. What do we need? Our health, money and provisions.
2. Life is about using your natural talents for the benefit of others as well as yourself.
3. And lastly, life is about creating memories.

And I'm happy to say that these three things have taken me on a good path towards a fulfilling life. Give it a try!

When you're with someone who is sharing their struggles with you...just smile at him/her and give them one of these. He/she will ask "What is that?" Then simply reply "Life Works in Threes."

Other titles coming out:

- Weight Struggles?
- Abundance Struggles?
- Parenting Struggles?
- Life Struggles?
- Purpose Struggles?
- Romance Struggles?
- Sales Struggles?
- Speaker Struggles?
- Time Struggles?
- Network Struggles?
- Marriage Struggles?
- Divorce Struggles?
- Money Struggles?
- Career Struggles?
- Dating Struggles?
- Caretaker Struggles?
- Forgiveness Struggles?
- Grieving Struggles?
- Success Struggles?
- Golf Struggles?
- Workplace Struggles?
- Stress Struggles?
- Shame/Guilt Struggles?
- Addiction Struggles?

Quotes about Happiness

"I once complained that I had no shoes until I met a man who had no feet." - Helen Keller

"Happiness is not the absence of problems, it's the ability to deal with them." - Steve Maraboli

"The happiest people don't have the best of everything, they make the best of everything." - Unknown

"Life is lived 'inside out' not 'outside in'. Material things and accolades are nice but not lasting. Decide to be happy no matter what." - Stephen Covey

"If you want a happy life, tie it to a goal, not people or things." - Albert Einstein

**If you want to be happy...
move from judgement to gratitude.**

63

When someone is struggling with a particular area or two, chances are they are "out of balance" with how life works. How does life work? Life works in threes.

If you're interested in personal topics like life, health, money or business topics like sales, time management and public speaking...TRYUNE WORKS! can shed some light on creating success in those areas.

The definition of TRIUNE is a group of three things; united. Being three in one, such as - humans are *mental, physical* and *spiritual beings.* The word TRYUNE is a play of the word TRIUNE, encouraging all to try this concept and help eliminate struggling unnecessarily.

LifeWorksInThrees.com